SIDE EFFECT OF THE NEW NORMAL

A Social Distancing Activity Book

For Parent And Children

TABLE OF CONTENTS

Chapter 1: What Is A Pandemic? 1

Chapter 2: What Is Social Distancing? 13

Chapter 3: Traditional School Vs New Teaching Methods
& E-Learning 24

Chapter4: Home Schooling 29

Ready Made Exercises 37

Conclusion 80

References 85

CHAPTER 1: WHAT IS A PANDEMIC?

According to the WHO (World Health Organization), a pandemic is the worldwide spread of a new disease.

An influenza pandemic occurs when a new influenza virus emerges and spreads around the world, and most people do not have immunity. Viruses that have caused past pandemics typically originated from animal influenza viruses. Some aspects of influenza pandemics can appear similar to seasonal influenza, while other characteristics may be quite different. For example, both seasonal and pandemic flu can cause infections in all age groups, and most cases will result in self-limited illness in which the person recovers fully without treatment. Typical seasonal influenza causes most of its deaths among the elderly, while other severe cases occur most commonly in people with a variety of medical conditions.

By contrast, this H1N1 pandemic caused most of its severe or fatal disease in younger people, including those with chronic conditions and healthy persons. It caused many more cases of viral pneumonia than is usually seen with seasonal influenza.

For both seasonal and pandemic influenza, the total number of people who get severely ill can vary. However, the impact or severity tends to be higher in pandemics because of the many people in the population who lack preexisting immunity to the new virus. When a large portion of the population is infected, even if the proportion of those infected that go on to develop the severe disease is small, the total number of severe cases can be quite large.

Also, for both seasonal and pandemic influenza, the highest levels of activity would be expected to occur in the usual influenza season period for an area. (In the temperate climate zones, this is usually the winter months, for example). But as was seen with the current H1N1 pandemic, pandemics can have unusual epidemiological patterns, and large outbreaks can occur in the summer months.

History of Pandemics

Over time, the human race has seen the emergence of different diseases and illnesses which have plagued humanity since the earliest days.

In this section, we look back at previous pandemics. Specifically, we investigate cholera, the Black Death, and the Spanish flu, among others. We will note any similarities and take lessons where we can.

1981 till present: HIV

With vast improvements in treatment, information, diagnostic capabilities, and surveillance in Western countries, it is easy to forget that experts still class HIV as a pandemic. Since the early 1980s, HIV has claimed the lives of more than 32 million people. At the end of 2018, around 37.9 million people were living with HIV. Although a virus causes HIV, HIV cannot transmit via coughs and sneezes. 2009-2010: H1N1 swine flu

According to the Centers for Disease Control and Prevention (CDC), between April 2009 and April 2010, the swine flu pandemic affected an estimated 60.8 million people. There were also around 274,304 hospitalizations and 12,469 deaths. Both swine flu and the novel coronavirus cause symptoms such as fever, chills, a cough, and headaches. Like SARS-CoV-2, the (H1N1) pdm09 virus was also significantly different from other strains. This meant that most people did not have any natural immunity.

Interestingly, some older adults had immunity, suggesting that (H1N1) pdm09 or something similar might have infected large numbers of people a few decades before. Because of this immunity, 80% of the fatalities occurred in people younger than 65. This isn't the case with SARS-CoV-2; all age groups seem to be equally likely to contract it, and older adults are most at risk of developing severe illness. Certain groups of people may have a level of immunity against SARS-CoV-2, but researchers have not yet identified such a group. The overall mortality rate of swine flu was around 0.02%.

The many returns of cholera

Over the past two centuries, cholera has reached pandemic proportions seven times. Experts class the cholera pandemic of 1961-1975 as the seventh one.

Cholera is a bacterial infection of the small intestine by certain strains of Vibrio cholera. It can be fatal within hours. The most common symptom is diarrhea, though muscle cramps and vomiting can also occur. Although immediate rehydration treatment is successful in up to 80% of cases, the mortality rate of cholera can be up to 50% without treatment. Cholera occurs when a person ingests contaminated food or water. The seventh pandemic was caused by a strain of V. cholera called El Tor, which scientists first identified in 1905. The outbreak appears to have begun on the island of Sulawesi in Indonesia. It spread to Bangladesh, India, and the Soviet Union, including Ukraine and Azerbaijan. By 1973, the outbreak had also reached Japan, Italy, and the South Pacific. In the 1990s, though the pandemic had officially ended, the same strain reached Latin America, a region that had not experienced cholera for 100 years. There, there were at least 400,000 cases and 4,000 deaths.

1918: The Spanish flu

In the spring of 1918, health professionals detected an H1N1 virus in United States military personnel. From January 1918 to December 1920, this virus — which appears to have moved from birds to humans — infected an estimated 500 million people. This equates to 1 in 3 people on Earth. The virus killed around 675,000 people in the U.S. alone and approximately 50 million worldwide. This strain of influenza, transmitted via respiratory droplets. The Spanish flu also impacted children under the age of 5 and adults aged 20-40.

A 25-year-old was more likely to die from the Spanish flu than a 74-year-old was. This is unusual for the flu. As with swine flu, it may be that older adults at this time had a preexisting immunity to a similar pathogen. Perhaps the 1889–1890 flu pandemic, or the Russian flu, afforded some protection to those who survived it.

Additionally, some scientists believe that younger people's vigorous immune responses might have led to more severe lung symptoms due to "exuberant pulmonary exudation." In other words, the strong immune reactions of young people may produce excess fluid in the lungs, making breathing even more difficult. At the time, there were no vaccines to prevent the disease and no antibiotics from treating the bacterial infections that sometimes developed alongside it. The virulent nature of this particular H1N1 strain and the lack of medication available made this the most severe pandemic in recent history. The pandemic came in two waves, with the second being more deadly than the first. However, rather abruptly, the virus disappeared.

A different time

The Spanish flu's high mortality rate was, in part, due to the virulence of the virus. Social differences also played a role. In 1918, people tended to live in close quarters and perhaps did not value hygiene as much. These factors can influence how quickly a virus spreads and how lethal it can be. Also, the world was at war, meaning that large numbers of troops were traveling to distant locations and aiding the spread. In peacetime, someone who is very ill will stay at home, whereas someone who is only a little under the weather might continue as normal. During World War I, malnutrition was common for both those at home and those on the frontline. This is yet another factor that may have made people more susceptible to disease.

The Spanish flu and physical distancing

The Spanish flu pandemic teaches us a valuable lesson about the effectiveness of quickly implementing physical distancing measures or social distancing measures. In Philadelphia, PA, officials downplayed the significance of the first cases in the city. Mass gatherings continued, and schools remained open. The city only implemented physical distancing and other measures around 14 days after the first cases appeared. This had significant consequences. In contrast, within two days of its first reported cases, St. Louis, MI, moved quickly to implement physical distancing measures.

Severe acute respiratory syndrome

In 2002, severe acute respiratory syndrome (SARS) became the first pandemic of the 21st century. Scientists believe that SARS-CoV-2 started in bats, moved into pangolins, then entered humans.

Similarly, SARS-CoV began in bats, but it went into civets before humans. SARS-CoV can transmit via droplets from coughs and sneezes. Globally, SARS infected an estimated 8,000 people in 29 countries and had a mortality rate of around 10%.

SARS affects older adults more severely than they do younger individuals. Around half of those over 65 who contracted SARS died, compared with just 1% of people under 24.

How was SARS eradicated?

In short, surveillance, the isolation of those who contracted it, and strict quarantine measures halted SARS' progress. As one paper puts it, "By interrupting all human-to-human transmission, SARS was eradicated."

The Black Death

No book on pandemics would be complete without mentioning the Black Death, also referred to as The Plague. Peaking in Europe between 1347 and 1351, the Black Death was responsible for an estimated 75–200 million deaths. It may have killed half of the entire population of Europe. The cause of this pandemic was a bacterium, called Yersinia pestis, rather than a virus. Epidemiologists believe that the Black Death also originated in Asia. However, the Black Death's march across the planet was spread by rodents rather than humans. Rodents carrying bacteria-infected fleas spread this disease. Y. pestis partially blocks the guts of fleas. As the fleas feed on a human, they attempt to clear their blocked bellies by regurgitating their meal. This effort releases Y.pestis into the vicinity of the flea's bite wound. Though much rarer, plague still exists, particularly in low-income regions. The majority of cases now occur in Africa. Thanks to improvements in medicine and hygiene, the disease has not reached pandemic proportions since the BlackDeath. Without treatment, the case-fatality ratio can be 30–100%. In the U.S., the mortality rate of the plague before antibiotics was 66%. By 1990–2010, modern medicine had reduced this figure to a still-high 11%. The Black Death pandemic eventually waned, and this seems to have been for a few reasons. People began to self-quarantine, and they stopped traveling as freely through fear of catching the disease. People also started to hold fragrant handkerchiefs against their mouths when in public, and this might have reduced the risk of infection and transmission.

What We Can Learn From Previous Pandemics

Pandemics have come and gone, but most importantly, they have left us with lessons on how to manage their spread.

"There are many examples where the lessons of the past are ignored," says Graham Mooney, a medicine historian at Johns Hopkins. For example, the government's reoccurring failure to anticipate and support citizens through the social and economic impacts of pandemics, from mandatory quarantines and travel restrictions to closing schools, workplaces, and local businesses. "These crises expose social inequality," Mooney said. Here's a quick look at what public health officials and epidemiologists have learned from past pandemics:

There are some key takeaways here.

1. Surveillance is essential — we need to know who is affected and who has been affected.

We have also learned that physical distancing and quarantine measures work. Where a pandemic happens, both geographically and historically, also makes a difference. Would the Black Death have been so devastating had the people of the time had access to modern medical treatments, an understanding of how germs spread, and improved nutrition? Probably not. It may be of little consolation, but it might help some of us, psychologically, to remember that we are not the only humans to have experienced such trials and tribulations — and we will not be the last.

Positive Outlook & Why We'll Get Through A Pandemic

A lot of people have witnessed their lives turn upside since the outbreak of this disease; social lives are on hold until further notice and anxiety are thriving on the unknown. Experts have discovered that loneliness and forced isolation are the primary cause of anxiety and depression in adults.

Despite all of this, keeping a positive mindset can go a long way in managing through a difficult time. While we try to distract ourselves from all the things happening at the moment, it is essential to try to divert your energy in focusing on the positive. According to The Evangelical Lutheran Good Samaritan Society's Senior pastor, Greg Wilcox -- "Having an attitude that looks for the positive, and tries to be optimistic. It can help you to filter out some of the constant barrages of bad or discouraging news — the figures of the disease and how it's growing. Holding onto that positive attitude can help you center on things that provide you with what you need to make it through the day. It's vital these days." According to an article on Forbes.com, on pandemics, the following tips have been provided.

1. **Limit your intake** - A person could watch 24-hour news channels, listen to different warnings on the radio, or visit different websites and be stuffed with the angst of the moment. Instead, it is advisable to choose a single news source and decide how much limited time you'll spend with it each day, then stick to that plan.

2. **Look to the past** - Getting hope from one's past resilience. A person may have likely endured other unforeseen major life disrupters like 9/11, major hurricanes, or the financial meltdown of 2008. But we made it through! And this had made us stronger. Knowing that you will get through, it is crucial to remind yourself of our resilience regularly.

3. **Watch a funny video** - Thanks to the massive popularity of YouTube, there are thousands of videos that can help you take your mind off current events, if only for three minutes at a time. Start to bookmark the funniest among them so you can return for a repeat viewing whenever things feel gloomy.

4. **Look after your neighbors-** You may be at low risk of severe consequences from the virus, but it may not be the same for your neighbors whose immune systems are compromised. The act of checking in on them (keeping six feet apart, of course) will not only make them feel good, but it will also make you feel good and remind you that there are others for whom this predicament is even more stressful.

Support your favorite local business. Maybe you're heeding the social distancing advice and aren't eager to sit in a crowded restaurant now. And others feel the same way. Those empty seats aren't helping the restaurant owner to pay her staff or keep the restaurant in business. Buy a gift card to assist the business owner now, and prepay for a wonderful meal you can have to celebrate when this pandemic is behind us.

Send gifts in the mail. It may not be wise to drop in on your loved ones with some fresh-baked goodies, so send them a card or present in the mail. Unexpected treats can be a pick-me-up-in time of stress. This is especially valuable to the elderly and grandparents who are living in nursing homes. Many facilities have closed their doors to all visitors, making residents feel even more isolated and vulnerable.

Take advantage of found time. I'm a public speaker, and my speaking gigs are canceling left and right. It's frustrating, and I could wallow in that for days. But that wouldn't be productive. These cancelations allow me to focus on some things I've had no time for and to accelerate my progress on other product offerings. It's liberating, and that's I've decided to shift my focus.

Practice or suggest random acts of kindness. Like leaving an envelope with a little gift for the Amazon Fresh delivery person who drops off your supplies outside your door. Or have a coffee delivered to your doorman. Your kindness doesn't require a monetary outlay. Write an unsolicited book review for a friend of yours who is an author. Comment on a colleague's LinkedIn post. Send a snail-mail note of appreciation to a friend or colleague. Many in the entire country of Italy broke out in song and applause to honor their healthcare workers. Thank the custodians in your building or workplace for their efforts to keep things safe. Think of those who could benefit from your thoughtfulness and generosity. Then act.

Take a daily inventory. Close your day, every day, with a positive acknowledgment of something you accomplished, learned, or are grateful for. It will help dilute some of the negativity you've absorbed and reminds you that not everything that's happening right now is terrible or depressing.

It is also important to remember that pandemics do end, and that modern science and medicine can be incredible forces for good. We no longer live in the Dark Ages; we are better armed today than we have ever been.

CHAPTER 2: WHAT IS SOCIAL DISTANCING?

Social distancing is a term employed by public health officials to deliberately put space between people to decrease how a disease spreads. One way to slow down the rapid spread of a virus is by social distancing. Also known as physical distancing, social distancing means keeping distance between oneself and people outside one's home. Also, canceling events that are likely to draw crowds is a form of social distancing. In a situation where a group is unavoidable or social distancing can't be practiced, it is advised to wear a face-covering cloth or a face mask - especially in places where community-based transmission is high.

According to the CDC, social distancing means:

- Remaining out of "congregate settings" as much as possible.
- Avoiding mass gatherings.
- Maintaining distance of about 6 feet from others when possible.

How Does Social Distancing Help Stop The Spread Of pandemics

Staying at least six feet apart from the next person will help reduce the spread of the virus. Working from home instead from at the office, home or online schooling, cancelling conferences or large meetings etc. are ways to practice social distancing which in turn prevents the spread if the virus. Taking appropriate measures like washing your hands regularly, including social or physical distancing, isolation and so on could help lessen the rate at which the infection spreads. One of the best ways to help stop the spread of a virus is to stay at home and only leave for essential needs. Social distancing is crucial for preventing the spread of contagious illnesses, especially those that can spread through coughing, sneezing and close contact. By minimizing the amount of close contact we have with others, we reduce our chances of catching the virus and spreading it to our loved ones and within our community.

1. Involve those who need to be included in your plan.

Talk with members of your household, your family, and friends to discuss your plan of action if an outbreak happens in your community. Take this time to determine what the needs of each person will be, and encourage those who take daily medications to stock up in case they are quarantined for some time.

2. Plan ways to care for loved ones at high-risk for complications.

Talk with high-risk loved ones and devise a plan for keeping them safe as well as a plan for if they become ill.

3. Create a list of local organizations that can help.

 Identify local information services, health care—including mental health care—, food services and other aid organizations in your community that you can contact.

Social distancing is an essential piece of the puzzle in slowing the outbreak, but there are other steps you can take to protect yourself and others.

4. Understand How It Spreads

A virus is thought to spread from person-to-person, between those who are within about 6 feet of one another. The virus can spread through respiratory droplets produced through coughs or sneezes, and these droplets can land in the mouths or noses of nearby people. The CDC also says these droplets can possibly be inhaled directly into the lungs.

5. Wash Your Hands (And Don't Touch Your Face).

Hand washing can protect against the spread of any virus or diseases and other illnesses. Wash your hands often with soap and water for at least 20 seconds, especially after being in a public place, after using the bathroom, before and after eating, after handling pets, and after blowing your nose, coughing, or sneezing. Remember: wet, lather, scrub, rinse, and dry. If soap and water are not available, opt for a hand sanitizer that contains at least 60 percent alcohol. Avoid touching your face with unwashed hands.

6. Clean and Disinfect.

Each day, you should clean and disinfect frequently-touched surfaces such as doorknobs, toilets, tables, light switches, countertops, handles, desks, faucets, sinks, and yes, even your phone.

7. Protect Others.

Even if you aren't exhibiting coronavirus symptoms, you might still carry it. Covering your mouth and nose with a tissue or the inside of your elbow when you cough or sneeze, especially avoiding contact with the elderly or immunosuppressed, and staying home.

How to interact with friends and extended family while Social Distancing

One of the consequences of social distancing is a strained relationship between family and friends - especially those who are far away. In instances like this, to maintain this relationship and also feel closer to friends and extended family, there is a need for constant interaction through frequent calls and text messages. A variety of games and interactive applications have been in use for communication with distant friends, such as Psych, draw something, house party, etc.

1. Psych!

Who can fake it best and fool the most people? That's the aim of Psych!, in which you all must come up with the most convincing false answer to trivia – such as what do you call a group of zebras? Each fake response is submitted anonymously alongside the real answer, leaving you and everyone else to pick the correct one. Get it right, you win a point, but also gain a point for every time someone else fell for your false answer. There are different categories to choose from and the ability to buy extension packs.

2. Draw Something

Test your drawing skills – and that of friends and family on Facebook – with Draw Something. The app will challenge you to draw something on your smartphone, which the other player must guess, and vice versa.

3. Words with Friends

This Scrabble-inspired game is ideal for word lovers, allowing you to play in pairs online. You can choose to download the app or find it directly within Facebook, by going to Menu and selecting Gaming, where there are several other titles to play.

4. Clash Royale

Prepare to battle opponents and defend your side against a friend in this real-time strategy video game. Protect your towers while storming your opponent's, as well as collecting cards and achievements along the way – but you will need to complete the training before you can set off.

5. Uno

Family classic Uno is brought to your smartphone, with the same principle as before. There's also the ability to take part in tournaments and work together in teams of two.

6. Houseparty

Houseparty, the video chat app which has exploded in popularity during the lockdown, features four different games to play, all while keeping the video conversation going in the background.

7. Remote Insensitivity

A game for the adults, Remote Insensitivity is essentially Cards against Humanity, with the same aim – create the most bizarre and crude sentences from a pack of statements. No need to download an app, just play online by visiting playingcards.io/game/remote-insensitivity and share the unique game code with others who wish to play. It's very manual, meaning you will need to deal cards and physically drag them, as well as keeping track of points yourself.

How Social Distancing Can Bring Families Closer Together

Social distancing doesn't mean your family can't still enjoy spending time with one another. Engaging in fun family activities every day can strengthen family bonds, relieve anxiety, and keep everyone sane and civil during this stressful period. While your family is gathered at home together, it's also an excellent time to create a household plan of action in case a pandemic outbreak happens in your community. The CDC recommends basing the details of your household plan on the needs and daily routine of your household members. Here are five different activities to do to come together as a family.

1. Get outside every day

If possible, go outdoors every day for a walk, family jog, or bike ride. You should ensure physical distancing if other people are around — maintain at least 6 feet between your family and other families.

Exercise allows children to burn energy, and its heart health benefits for grown-ups can't be beaten.

2. Play and exercise indoors

When going outside isn't possible due to the weather or social distancing requirements, schedule several play times throughout the day. Athletic activities like hula-hooping, jumping rope, and shooting baskets with soft foam balls provide fun entertainment while also elevating your heart rate.

You can also teach your kids more adult exercises, like yoga or bodyweight workouts. Role modeling fitness for your kids will create a healthy mindset; they'll carry forward into adulthood.

3. Plan and cook healthy recipes together

Get your children involved in meal planning by sitting down every couple of days to plan the next day's menu. Browse recipes at websites like the American Heart Association or the government's ChooseMyPlate site. When everyone agrees on a meal, work together in the kitchen to cook it. Children can perform age-appropriate tasks like measuring ingredients or peeling potatoes. Cooking provides a fun family activity and equips your kids with skills they need to make healthy food choices throughout their lives.

4. Spring clean your home

If you must be confined indoors, make the time productive by doing a good spring cleaning. Tackle one room or area per day and clean it from top to bottom.

Younger kids can dust and vacuum and sort through their toys and clothes to determine what to keep and what to donate or throw away.

Older children can disinfect high-touch surfaces, scrub baseboards, and even touch up paint. By the time the pandemic passes, your home will look like new.

5. Substitute craft projects for screen time

It may be tempting to let kids indulge in lots of screen time so you can work from home, but staring at a smartphone or tablet for hours may not be the healthiest option.

Instead, schedule some craft projects that all of you can do together. You can order age-appropriate craft kits that deliver everything you need right to your door. Here are just a few project ideas: painting (finger painting for the little ones), model building, origami, and coloring. If you can't afford to craft supplies right now, a quick search online will reveal hundreds of websites that offer free instructions for craft projects that use common household supplies, like discarded egg cartons and boxes. By limiting screen time and replacing it with craft projects, you may discover a budding Picasso in your family.

Using this time of social distancing to focus on building new healthy family habits can bring you and your children closer. It can also help to create new lifestyle patterns that keep you all healthy moving forward.

How Social Distancing Can Help With Internal Growth

Social distancing and isolation can be challenging.

"Don't underestimate the personal trauma, and don't underestimate the pain of isolation. It is real," Cuomo said. "This is not the human condition — not to be comforted, not to be close, to be afraid, and you can't hug someone. ... This is all unnatural and disorienting." - Andrew Cuomo

Elena Mikalsen, chief of the Psychology Section at Children's Hospital of San Antonio, said that it is helpful that the entire world is basically in the same situation. This commonality is leading to the rapid development of coping strategies from multiple sources, including friends, schools, and businesses. During this period, Mikalsen is advising her patients to stay connected with people, exercise regularly, and keep to a schedule, so everybody in the household has some purpose in their day. Waiting around and worrying about getting sick can lead to increased anxiety. A key factor driving people's decisions on whether to isolate could come down to personality.

Extroverts have this strong need to always be around other people. The idea of being in a quiet place with no entertainment is hugely anxiety-provoking," Mikalsen said. "Versus, you know, an introvert is perfectly happy in a tiny little room with nothing. You can lock up an introvert in a New York City apartment and have them not come out for two months, and they'll be perfectly happy."

Dealing With Negative Emotions and Side Effects Of Social Distancing

As mentioned earlier, fear, anxiety, and stress are all adverse side effects of social distancing, which may lead to adverse psychological effects on our bodies. It is therefore essential to employ mechanisms or ways to help us cope with these effects;

1. Observe and describe your emotions in a nonjudgmental way.

Some people naturally run hotter than others when it comes to experiencing strong emotions like anxiety. This strategy entails observing your surroundings or circumstance and then describing your observations in words. Think along the lines of a reporter. The purpose of this technique is to calm down strong emotions so you can reason and act more skillfully. For most of us, it's impossible to reason when we're emotional.

2. Have a distress tolerance plan.

We're all experiencing anxiety with today's new realities. Having a distress tolerance plan in place for calming down strong emotions is beneficial for taking care of our emotional health. A distress plan can include making time for taking warm baths, watching funny movies, playing games on your iPhone, or exercising. These are all great ways to calm down strong emotions, so our rational brains can take over.

3. Take regular and frequent breaks from watching, reading, or listening to the news. Being exposed to information 24/7 about the pandemic is not only emotionally upsetting, but it's also bad for our physical health. Research studies show that exposure to prolonged periods of stress can lead to physical symptoms, including headaches, stomach issues, headaches, elevated blood pressure, cardiac disease, and problems sleeping.

4. Take care of your body.

Try to eat healthy, well-balanced meals, exercise regularly, get plenty of sleep, and avoid alcohol and drugs. Studies analyzed in

JAMA (The Journal of The Medical Association) showed that meditation does help manage anxiety. The focus of mindfulness meditation is to train the brain to stay in the moment, which, in turn, decreases our stress levels.

5. Create meaningful interactions with your family.

Although a pandemic is not what one would ever hope for, try to take advantage of the extra time you might have for connecting with your children, partner, pets, and friends. Playing board games, cards, and watching movies together are great ways to deepen connections and create memories, even during stressful times.

6. Use social networking sites and virtual platforms for staying connected.

In addition to texting, I've been using FaceTime to connect to friends and family while practicing social distancing. Seeing the other person's facial expressions and hearing their voice creates a deeper, fuller, and richer social interaction. Deeper and richer social interactions help to combat depression or loneliness brought on by social distancing.

7. Connect with nature.

As much as possible, go for a walk, a run or a bike ride. Research consistently shows that connecting with nature decreases symptoms associated with anxiety and depression.

CHAPTER 3: TRADITIONAL SCHOOL VS NEW TEACHING METHODS & E-LEARNING

Teaching styles have changed significantly over the years. The traditional way that education was delivered was through recitation and memorization techniques, whereas the modern way of doing things involves interactive methods. The back-to-basics traditional education method, also known as conventional education, is still widely used in schools. The old-fashioned way of teaching was all about recitation. For example, students would sit in silence, while one student after another would take turns to recite the lesson until each one had been called. The teacher would listen to each student's recitation, and they were expected to study and memorize the assignments. At the end of the module, a written or verbal exam would be conducted; this process was called an Assignment Study Recitation Test.

How traditional methods were taught ensured that students were rewarded for their efforts, used class periods efficiently, and exercised clear rules to manage students' behavior. They were based on established customs that had been used successfully in schools over many years. The teachers communicated the knowledge and enforced standards of conduct.

Education reforms mean that learning is taught from a completely different angle. Progressive educational practices focus more on the individual student's needs than if all students are at the same level of understanding. The modern way of teaching is more activity-based, using questioning, explaining, demonstration, and collaboration techniques.

One modern method is spaced learning. This is when students are encouraged to quickly switch through activities, such as providing 10 minutes of knowledge on a subject with a PowerPoint presentation and then having 15 minutes of playtime. Spaced learning aims to achieve better grades, and it works! This is said to be more effective than teaching students by traditional methods for four hours, thus helping the brain cells to create connections that they need to remember knowledge. It also helps people relax.

Sonia Jackson, wrote an interesting blog post about modern teaching methods for Getting Smart states: "The traditional "chalk and talk" method of teaching that's persisted for hundreds of years is now producing inferior results when compared with the more modern and revolutionary teaching methods that are available for use in schools today. Greater student interaction is encouraged, the boundaries of authority are broken down, and enjoyment over grades is emphasized."

The interactivity and communication offered in class-based lessons can still be missing in online learning and traditional teaching. Because conventional techniques used repetition and memorization of information to educate students, it meant that they were not developing critical thinking, problem-solving, and decision-making skills. Modern learning encourages students to collaborate and therefore be more productive.

Challenges with New Methods

Teaching is getting more and more complex and challenging these days. Students' patience level is decreasing, while rudeness, argumentation, disobedience, and short temper are on the rise. Is it due to modern age competition, stress, availability of alternate sources of knowledge like the internet or violence shown in movies, T.V. series', and video games?

Understanding The Importance Of E-Learning

Today, the use of the web to teach and learn is inevitable for both teachers and students. Online courses are becoming more and more necessary for education to and for knowledge spread. Thus, teachers should consider this trend in education and prepare technically and pedagogically to consider online teaching. In turn, students need to get enough skills to help them effectively benefit from the advantages e-learning provides.

Today, e-learning is adopted not only by students but also by organizations that want to offer training for their employees. E-learning is a priority for businesses that look forward to improving employee skills and the economic benefits they can generate from that. That's why online learning has become an essential factor for both education and business.

Having Space To Yourself When E-Learning

Learning online requires determination because no teacher is keeping an eye on you, and distractions are just everywhere. A good starting point is creating a pleasant environment to learn in. Here are a few recommendations that could help with your e-learning:

1. Make space

Stacks of paper and books might look impressive, but a sudden book avalanche is a distraction at best and a hazard at worst. Make sure you have plenty of room for the device you're learning on and an area to take notes if required. Clear your immediate working area of clutter and distractions, and you should be able to improve your focus.

2. Get the temperature right

The next distraction to remove is temperature. Make sure you're not too hot or cold. If you find yourself shivering (or sweating) over your computer at home, try visiting a local library or cafe, their temperature is usually constant.

3. Adjust the lights

Like temperature, how much light you want when studying can sometimes come down to personal preference: maybe you like a room as full of natural light as possible, or maybe you prefer it cozy and dark. Either way make sure you're able to clearly see your screen and there's not too much glare, else you might end up with eye strain.

4. Get comfortable

If you're using a computer for an extended period of time, making sure your computer is positioned appropriately and that you're sitting appropriately. How do you do that? Read more on the NHS to find out. If you're in an uncomfortable seat or position, you're not going to be able to focus on your studies, so try and make yourself as comfortable as possible (without falling asleep).

5. Turn up (or down) the volume

When you're doing an online course, you're probably going to have videos to watch, so music isn't always useful. But if you've got reading to do, an assignment to write or notes to organize might spur you on. Work out if music helps you, and then investigate if certain music genres are better than others. Sometimes lyrics can be distracting, so try searching for lyric-free playlists.

6. Learn what works for you

Lastly, and most importantly, you need to learn what works for you. Maybe you learn best amongst the clutter in the heat of the summer sun. Perhaps you learn exceptionally well listening to 90s club anthems. Treat our advice as a starting point and try adjusting your environment; eventually, you should find something that works for you.

CHAPTER4: HOME SCHOOLING

In plain terms, homeschooling means learning outside the private or public school environment. Just like the phrase 'work from home', homeschooling means getting access to school education without actually being in a proper school. Parents.Com describes homeschooling as a 'progressive movement around the country and the world, in which parents educate their children at home instead of sending them to a traditional public or private school.' Families have different reasons for homeschooling their kids. While homeschooling doesn't necessarily mean 'schooling at home,' for most families, it means going out and about each day, learning from the rich resources of the community, and interacting with other homeschoolers. The parents or guardians of the students are committed to monitoring and overseeing such a child's educational development.

Homeschooling is one of the world's fastest-moving educational movement. It is not so different from traditional schooling in that it also involves lots of detailed curriculum and bookwork. Using tutors and group classes, as well as activities like scouting or everyday activities, parents or guardians can handle home education as efficiently as possible.

How homeschooling is necessary during these times

Homeschooling isn't really necessary in this period. However, parents are first advised to teach their children life skills instead. Keeping kids in touch with their academics from time to time is a preferable way to teach them. Homeschooling is an intentional act, and it requires steadfast commitment from a parent- who also works from home.

According to John Holt, author of the best-selling book Teach Your Own, the most important thing parents need to homeschool their children is "to like them, enjoy their company, their physical presence, their energy, foolishness, and passion. They have to enjoy all their talk and questions, and enjoy equally trying to answer those questions." For the majority of parents who homeschool, the only prerequisite is the desire to do so, along with a dedication to the educational process.

Making It Easier For Parents To Home School

While this isn't a typical or ideal homeschooling experience, it can provide an opportunity to nurture family relationships, explore new interests and skills, and get a glimpse of education without schooling.

Be a role model: It is essential to put yourself in a place where your kids see you as a role model. Children will react to and follow your reactions. They learn from your example.

1. Set up a dedicated school room:

The dining room table makes a great gathering space for school work. The kids won't mind eating in the living room for a while, and the dedicated space will start to feel like a learning place.

2. Experiment:

Nothing beats experiential learning. There are so many incredible scientific experiments that you can perform with household items and minimal supplies. Our favorite science website is ScienceBob.com. His experiments on the Jimmy Fallon show are remarkable and hysterical!

3. Go off on tangents:

If your child is interested in a topic, explore it in more depth. An internet search revealed a lost purple pigment currently being analyzed for new applications in high-speed train technology and the development of quantum computers.

4. Don't be afraid to walk away:

When you get frustrated or lose your patience, take a break. The amount of material you will cover while homeschooling will be much greater than that covered in a typical school day.

5. Exercise: For at least an hour per day, go outside.

During our homeschool years together, my children biked, ran trails, walked on the beach, or just played in the yard daily. Now, it is part of their lifestyle. Establishing healthy habits early sets the stage for a lifetime of wellness.

6. Put family first:

Being successful academically is essential, but take care of each other above all else. Being together always means sharing the good and bad. We've faced severe illnesses, loss, and many happy times together.

*Remember, you have everything you need at your fingertips:

The internet offers a vast network of support for every academic subject imaginable.

Being thrust into homeschooling amid a pandemic isn't easy. But with a little preparation, you can make this a positive experience for both you and your kids.

The importance of Keeping The Relationship With Teachers and Fellow Classmates

1. TRY TO SAY HELLO FREQUENTLY, IF YOU CAN

Try to make sure your kids know you are thinking of them, care for them, and miss them. For kids with access to technology, simple daily hellos via video might be the only time the student sees the teacher on some days—and that sense of connection is vital to sustain.

For students without internet connectivity, try calling by phone; consider rotating through small groups of students each day to make this a more manageable task. "Taking the time to reach out and call each kid takes forever," says sixth- and eighth-grade English teacher Cathleen Beach board, but she sees a big impact: "The first few days, I had only a few kids logging on, but now I have almost 98 percent attendance," she says.

2. HOW TO MAINTAIN MORNING MEETINGS

Routines that foster connection are a core part of classroom life, and finding ways for students to experience these at home will help ease students' transition to home-based learning.

Margaret Shafer, a third-grade teacher, has kids respond to daily prompts during her morning meetings. Kids can see each other's responses and react if they want to. "My relationships with my students are part of my instruction, and their relationships with each other are critical to their enjoyment of school," she says, underscoring the fact that maintaining relationships is not an afterthought. "So when I planned (very quickly!) to start distance learning, the first thing I wanted to begin as a way to comfort the kids and let them know that I still care about them and their friends are still out there."

3. REIMAGINE TEMPERATURE CHECKS

For example, routine, informal check-ins—roses and thorns or selecting an emoji to match your mood—shouldn't fall by the wayside. Keep it quick and simple: "I posted on Schoology to give me a thumbs up, thumbs sideways (meh), or thumbs down to describe their day.... I encourage them to take selfies of their thumbs," says high school teacher Javier Rivera via Twitter.

Finally, some teachers are using forms, like this one created by the Association for Middle-Level Education, as a quick, asynchronous way to get kids to tell you how they're feeling that day.

4. TRY SNAIL-MAIL PEN PALS, PHONE PALS, OR VIRTUAL TURN AND TALK

We learn better in social contexts. For many students, transitioning to learning from home is complicated by the impact of being cut off from peers—even though many older students might communicate with friends via social media and texting.

If technology doesn't allow, we can create pen pals or other paper-and-pen activities by sending home envelopes, paper, and stamps if your school is able. Or mimic 'turn and talk' by setting up phone pals where students call each other on the phone several times a week to discuss specific topics or prompts.

5. CREATE VIRTUAL TABLES (BUT DON'T JUST GROUP FRIENDS)

For older kids, teachers can set up virtual table groups. Google Classroom can be used for this, especially if the students are already familiar with the platform.

Though many kids will stay in touch with their circle of friends, it's important to think about pairing kids with peers who aren't in their immediate social circle—and then mix up the groups weekly.

6. CONSIDER INCLUDING PARENTS

Students are asked to invite a parent online, allowing the adults to ask questions, express concerns, or request advice.

7. GET KIDS TO NAME—AND PROCESS—THEIR OWN EMOTIONS

Writing assignments, says Short, the English teacher, offer students valuable opportunities to process the complex mix of emotions they may be experiencing as a result of their upended routines and schedules, social isolation, and the challenges of being cooped up at home.

Coping with Missing Teachers

In many ways, pandemics become an unprecedented test for teacher-student relationships, forcing a readjustment of expectations without daily check-ins and in-person interaction, without tissues for tears, high-fives for a job well done or praise in front of classmates. Of course, teachers want their students to master content, develop a love of learning, and move on to the next grade. But these teachers also know that success requires time and trusting relationships.

READY MADE EXERCISES

Social Distancing Word Search

Search the words given below and circle them.

```
D I S E A S E T A T S E M E F L A Q
S A N I T I Z E T E E I I U I A T U
A E T P E N S M S P L I N P S W T A
U J L O E S E L F R A R E R E S D R
L A Y C M R O R F E C V F O L A O A
A V O I D G T T O V A E U T F F N N
C O V I D P S C H E R T L E E E I T
L P M O R E P O O N E S L C S I T I
E M O T I O R A L T H O G T T C E N
W N R T T H E R A I Y R E I E T E E
E O S A V O A A D O T P S O E I N Y
S O C I A L D O L N Y M E N S I C K
```

Social   Spread
COVID   Disease
Quarantine   Protection
Sanitize   Avoid
Self care   Safe
Sick   Prevention

What were your thoughts regarding this activity before you started it?

What did you learn about yourself after completing this activity?

On a scale of 1 - 10; With 1 — being easy to complete and 10 — being difficult to complete how would you rate this activity?

Why did you give this activity this rating?

What emotions did you experience?

After completing this activity, what is one action step that you will put in place?

Social Distancing Maze

Help your way out through the maze away from the social gathering.

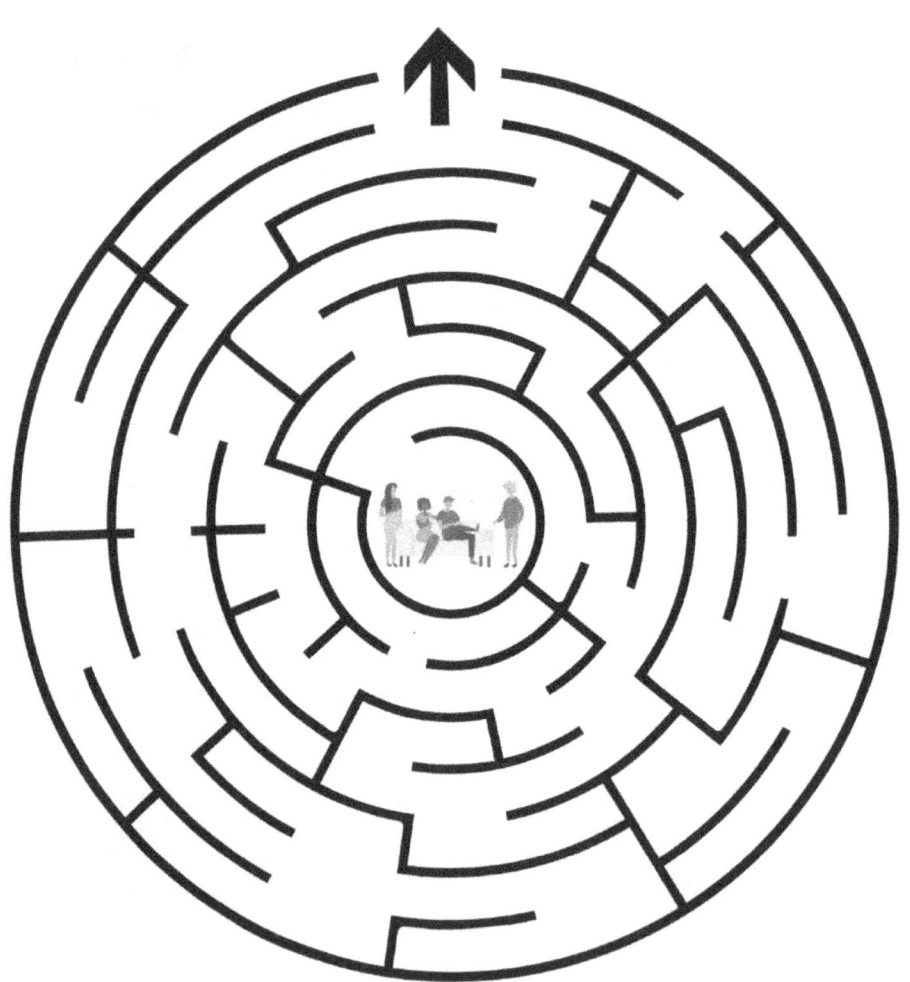

What were your thoughts regarding this activity before you started it?

What did you learn about yourself after completing this activity?

On a scale of 1 - 10; With 1 — being easy to complete and 10 — being difficult to complete how would you rate this activity?

Why did you give this activity this rating?

What emotions did you experience?

After completing this activity, what is one action step that you will put in place?

Days of Caring

> In this pandemic, we should not forget those who are needy. We can give charity to provide help and raise money for those in need.

If you have $100 to give to a charity, which one would you choose? Circle your choice.

Write in the lines below. Give atleast two reasons why you chose your choice.

What were your thoughts regarding this activity before you started it?

What did you learn about yourself after completing this activity?

On a scale of 1 - 10; With 1 — being easy to complete and 10 — being difficult to complete how would you rate this activity?

Why did you give this activity this rating?

What emotions did you experience?

After completing this activity, what is one action step that you will put in place?

What were your thoughts regarding this activity before you started it?

What did you learn about yourself after completing this activity?

On a scale of 1 - 10; With 1 — being easy to complete and 10 — being difficult to complete how would you rate this activity?

Why did you give this activity this rating?

What emotions did you experience?

After completing this activity, what is one action step that you will put in place?

Quarantine Story Writing Time

Write an interesting story/experience of yourself while living in quarantine.

What were your thoughts regarding this activity before you started it?

What did you learn about yourself after completing this activity?

On a scale of 1 - 10; With 1 — being easy to complete and 10 — being difficult to complete how would you rate this activity?

Why did you give this activity this rating?

What emotions did you experience?

After completing this activity, what is one action step that you will put in place?

Quarantine Crafts

Cut and string the lights to add some cheer to your home.

What were your thoughts regarding this activity before you started it?

What did you learn about yourself after completing this activity?

On a scale of 1 - 10; With 1 — being easy to complete and 10 — being difficult to complete how would you rate this activity?

Why did you give this activity this rating?

What emotions did you experience?

After completing this activity, what is one action step that you will put in place?

Quarantine Checklist

- ○ Use mask
- ○ Clean the surfaces
- ○ Eat healthy
- ○ Maintain a safe distance
- ○ Cover your mouth
- ○ Stay at home
- ○ Don't touch your face
- ○ Wash your hands regularly
- ○ Do some exercise

What were your thoughts regarding this activity before you started it?

What did you learn about yourself after completing this activity?

On a scale of 1 - 10; With 1 — being easy to complete and 10 — being difficult to complete how would you rate this activity?

Why did you give this activity this rating?

What emotions did you experience?

After completing this activity, what is one action step that you will put in place?

Social Distancing Do's And Don'ts

In social distancing, there are certain do's and don'ts in order to protect ourselves from contracting coronavirus. Draw an arrow to the correct illustration.

What were your thoughts regarding this activity before you started it?

What did you learn about yourself after completing this activity?

On a scale of 1 - 10; With 1 — being easy to complete and 10 — being difficult to complete how would you rate this activity?

Why did you give this activity this rating?

What emotions did you experience?

After completing this activity, what is one action step that you will put in place?

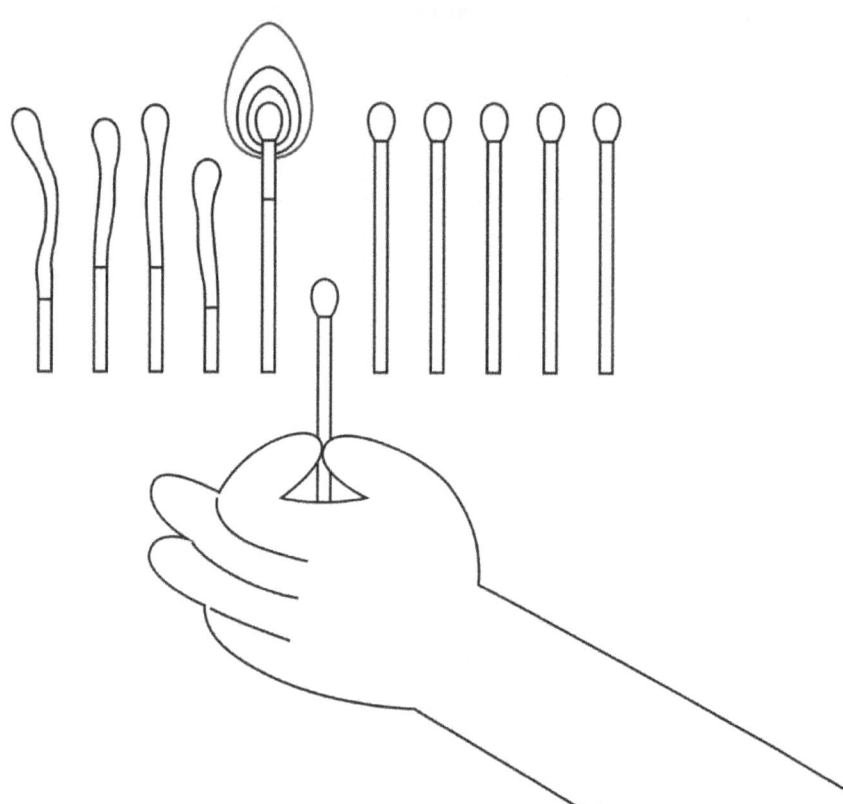

What were your thoughts regarding this activity before you started it?

What did you learn about yourself after completing this activity?

On a scale of 1 - 10; With 1 — being easy to complete and 10 — being difficult to complete how would you rate this activity?

Why did you give this activity this rating?

What emotions did you experience?

After completing this activity, what is one action step that you will put in place?

Social Distancing Daily Routine

List out some activities that are part of your daily routine while social distancing.

- Family Activities
- Chores
- Free Play
- Evening Activities
- Morning Work
- Daily Menu

What were your thoughts regarding this activity before you started it?

What did you learn about yourself after completing this activity?

On a scale of 1 - 10; With 1 — being easy to complete and 10 — being difficult to complete how would you rate this activity?

Why did you give this activity this rating?

What emotions did you experience?

After completing this activity, what is one action step that you will put in place?

Boredome Busting Bingo

Make multiple copies of the bingo given below, cut out the pieces and play with your siblings during quarantine.

Read a book	Play a board game	Sanitize all door knobs	Listen to the music	Make a meal
Draw a picture	Water the plants	Do a workout	Build something	Play a video game
Write a note to loved one	Play Tic-Tac-Toe	Art Hub	Pick 5 toys to give away	Make a chalk drawing
Clean your room	Blow bubbles	Fold clothes	Write a story	Call a grandparent
Help with chores	Put a puzzle together	Build a tower of cups	Sing a song	Play with pet

What were your thoughts regarding this activity before you started it?

What did you learn about yourself after completing this activity?

On a scale of 1 - 10; With 1 — being easy to complete and 10 — being difficult to complete how would you rate this activity?

Why did you give this activity this rating?

What emotions did you experience?

After completing this activity, what is one action step that you will put in place?

Daily Quarantine Questions

What am I GRATEFUL FOR today?

Who am I checking in on OR connecting with today?

What expectations of NORMAL am I letting go of today?

How am I moving my BODY today?

How can I be CREATIVE today?

What were your thoughts regarding this activity before you started it?

What did you learn about yourself after completing this activity?

On a scale of 1 - 10; With 1 — being easy to complete and 10 — being difficult to complete how would you rate this activity?

Why did you give this activity this rating?

What emotions did you experience?

After completing this activity, what is one action step that you will put in place?

What were your thoughts regarding this activity before you started it?

What did you learn about yourself after completing this activity?

On a scale of 1 - 10; With 1 — being easy to complete and 10 — being difficult to complete how would you rate this activity?

Why did you give this activity this rating?

What emotions did you experience?

After completing this activity, what is one action step that you will put in place?

Quarantine Calendar

Plan your quarantine period calendar by numbering the boxes from 1 to 30. Write your own ideas in the empty boxes.

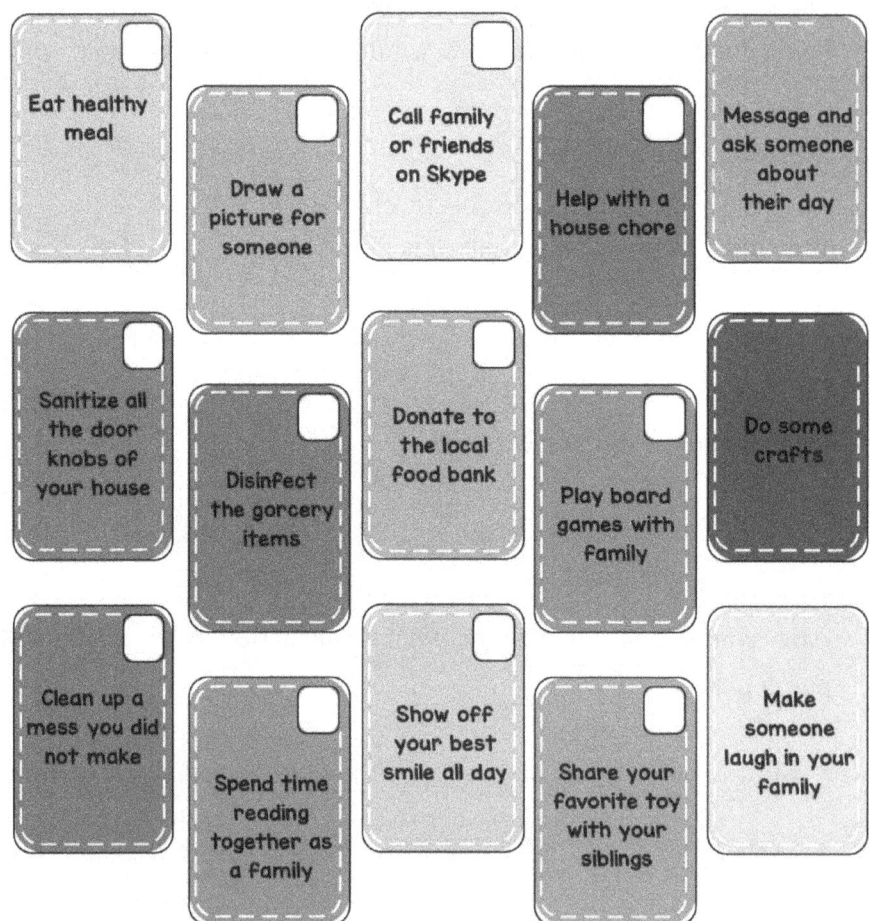

- Eat healthy meal
- Draw a picture for someone
- Call family or friends on Skype
- Help with a house chore
- Message and ask someone about their day
- Sanitize all the door knobs of your house
- Disinfect the gorcery items
- Donate to the local food bank
- Play board games with family
- Do some crafts
- Clean up a mess you did not make
- Spend time reading together as a family
- Show off your best smile all day
- Share your favorite toy with your siblings
- Make someone laugh in your family

What were your thoughts regarding this activity before you started it?

What did you learn about yourself after completing this activity?

On a scale of 1 - 10; With 1 — being easy to complete and 10 — being difficult to complete how would you rate this activity?

Why did you give this activity this rating?

What emotions did you experience?

After completing this activity, what is one action step that you will put in place?

Quarantine Calendar

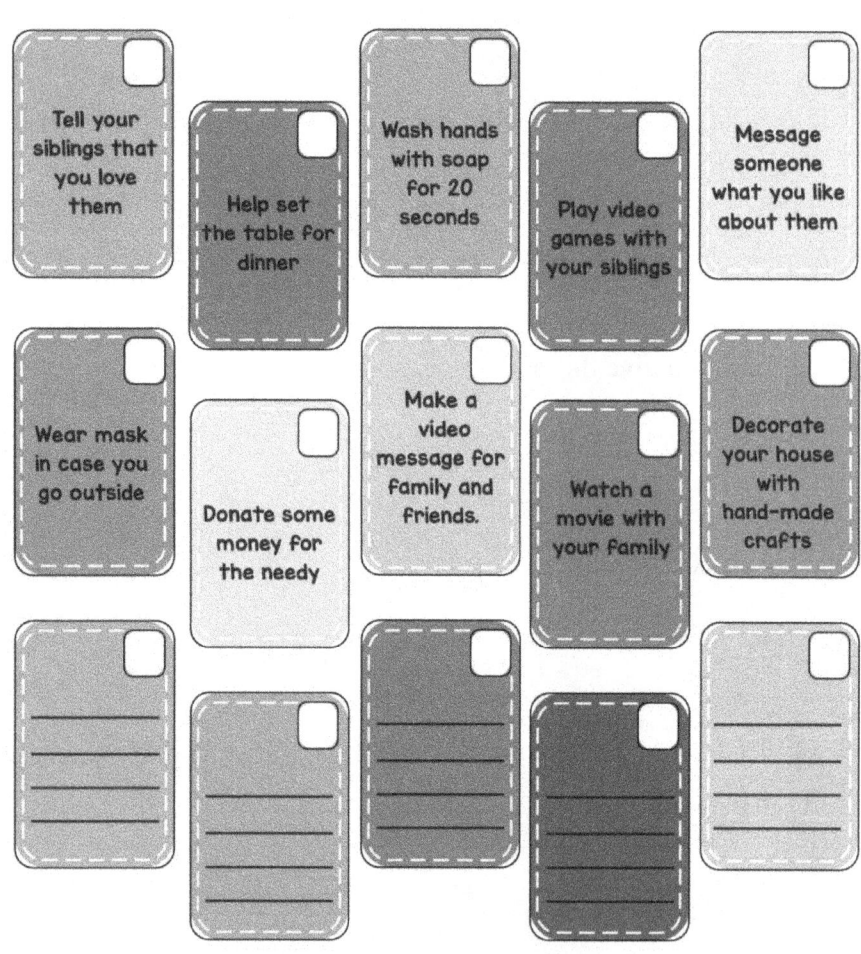

What were your thoughts regarding this activity before you started it?

What did you learn about yourself after completing this activity?

On a scale of 1 - 10; With 1 — being easy to complete and 10 — being difficult to complete how would you rate this activity?

Why did you give this activity this rating?

What emotions did you experience?

After completing this activity, what is one action step that you will put in place?

Quarantine Routine

YOU ARE NOT STUCK AT HOME, YOU ARE SAFE AT HOME!

WHAT AM I DOING TO KEEP BUSY:

What were your thoughts regarding this activity before you started it?

What did you learn about yourself after completing this activity?

On a scale of 1 - 10; With 1 — being easy to complete and 10 — being difficult to complete how would you rate this activity?

Why did you give this activity this rating?

What emotions did you experience?

After completing this activity, what is one action step that you will put in place?

Quarantine Icebreakers

Below are some activities / icebreakers that you can play with your family while living in quarantine.

1. Word Association

Ask the group to sit in a circle. The first person starts with any word they wish i.e. red. The next person repeats the first word and adds another word which links to the first i.e. tomato. The next person repeats the previous word and add another word link i.e. soup, and so on. To keep this moving, only allow five seconds for each word link.

2. Around the World

The leader begins by saying the name of any country, city, river, ocean or mountain that can be found in an atlas. The young person next to him must then say another name that begins with the last letter of the word just given. Each person has a definite time limit (e.g. three seconds) and no names can be repeated. For example – First person: London, Second Person: Niagara Falls, Third Person: Switzerland.

3. Backward Clumps

Divide into pairs. Ask each pair to sit on the floor with their partner, backs together, feet out in front and arms linked. Their task is to stand up together. Once everyone has done this, two pairs join together and the group of four try to repeat the task. After they succeed, add another two and try again. Keep adding people until your whole group is trying to stand together. A sight to behold!

What were your thoughts regarding this activity before you started it?

What did you learn about yourself after completing this activity?

On a scale of 1 - 10; With 1 — being easy to complete and 10 — being difficult to complete how would you rate this activity?

Why did you give this activity this rating?

What emotions did you experience?

After completing this activity, what is one action step that you will put in place?

Social Distancing Color Time

What were your thoughts regarding this activity before you started it?

What did you learn about yourself after completing this activity?

On a scale of 1 - 10; With 1 — being easy to complete and 10 — being difficult to complete how would you rate this activity?

Why did you give this activity this rating?

What emotions did you experience?

After completing this activity, what is one action step that you will put in place?

Time Capsule Worksheet

Days spent INSIDE:

What has been the BIGGEST CHANGE?

How are you finding HOMESCHOOLING?

How are you FEELING?

Your top 3 MOMENTS from this experience:

What were your thoughts regarding this activity before you started it?

What did you learn about yourself after completing this activity?

On a scale of 1 - 10; With 1 — being easy to complete and 10 — being difficult to complete how would you rate this activity?

Why did you give this activity this rating?

What emotions did you experience?

After completing this activity, what is one action step that you will put in place?

Collective Wellbeing Quarantine Checklist

	S	M	T	W	T	F	S
I played, moved, or did some physical activity.	○	○	○	○	○	○	○
I connected with someone.	○	○	○	○	○	○	○
I meditated, journaled, or took time for reflection.	○	○	○	○	○	○	○
I learned something new.	○	○	○	○	○	○	○
I undertook an act of service.	○	○	○	○	○	○	○
I drank 2 – 3 litres of water.	○	○	○	○	○	○	○
I set a small goal and achieved it.	○	○	○	○	○	○	○

What were your thoughts regarding this activity before you started it?

What did you learn about yourself after completing this activity?

On a scale of 1 - 10; With 1 — being easy to complete and 10 — being difficult to complete how would you rate this activity?

Why did you give this activity this rating?

What emotions did you experience?

After completing this activity, what is one action step that you will put in place?

Would You Rather...

Would you rather... be able to teleport anywhere or be able to read minds?

Would you rather... be the first person to explore a planet or be a drug inventor that cures a deadly disease?

Would you rather... relive the same day for 365 days or lose a year of your life?

Would you rather... never be able to eat meat or never be able to eat vegetables?

Would you rather... be poor but help people or become incredibly rich by hurting people?

Would you rather... lose all of your money and valuables or all of the pictures you have ever taken?

Would you rather... I live your entire life in a virtual reality where all your wishes are granted or in the real world?

Would you rather... be held in high regard by your parents or your friends?

What were your thoughts regarding this activity before you started it?

What did you learn about yourself after completing this activity?

On a scale of 1 - 10; With 1 — being easy to complete and 10 — being difficult to complete how would you rate this activity?

Why did you give this activity this rating?

What emotions did you experience?

After completing this activity, what is one action step that you will put in place?

CONCLUSION

We're All In This Together.

Remember, you're not alone. We can all get affected by pandemics, and most of us will experience an increase in our stress levels. It's unavoidable. Simply knowing we're all in this together and nobody is alone can help reduce feelings of loneliness.

List of Social Distancing Activities To Do With Family

As families across the country encounter the reality of life in lockdown, it is crucial to find ways to remain stimulated and entertained and avoid being glued to screens all day. From at-home workouts to crafts and virtual, cultural entertainment experiences, we put together an essential list of ways to ensure you and your family remain stimulated, happy, and joyful in the coming weeks.

Implement a routine

It can be tough to maintain a routine for both adults and children when you face an entire day spent in the house. However, both you and your kids are used to following a schedule. Mapping out everyone's responsibilities and activities for the day helps keep things structured.

Tour the world's leading museums

Although the coronavirus has limited your ability to travel, you can still visit cultural sites online using Google Arts and Culture. The tech company has 3,468 virtual museum tours from around the world, along with history and context for many pieces of art. Some of the museums you can tour include the Louvre in Paris, the Guggenheim Museum in New York, The British Museum in London, the Acropolis in Athens, the Vatican in Rome and The Smithsonian in Washington.

Board games & puzzles

There's nothing better than a challenging puzzle or good old-fashioned board game. Loved by both young and old, these are an ideal way to pass the time as a family. Sales of board games and jigsaw puzzles soared by 240% during the first official week of coronavirus lockdown in the U.K., according to The Guardian. Check out some great board games and puzzles here (if you're prepared to wait for delivery).

Baking and cooking

Lockdown provides the ideal opportunity to hone your and your family's cooking skills. Cooking is comforting, brings families together and teaches valuable life skills. Come up with theme days to create a sense of fun and excitement, collectively cook a delicious family meal, allow your children to experiment in the kitchen, and let your kids help your meal plan.

Get Active

Getting active not only improves physical health but can have a significant impact on our mental health. Make exercise in your home a daily family affair. There are hundreds of apps and websites offering both free and paid exercise streaming options from yoga, to Pilates to dancing. If you're prepared to wait, we've got some great merchant partners who offer awesome gear for home workouts. Check out the health & fitness section of our store directory.

Go on a virtual game drive.

Duma Private Game Reserve in the Sabi Sand is offering two game drives per day, which viewers can watch live on YouTube. The morning drive is from 5:30 until 8:30 am, and the afternoon drive is from 3:30 until 6:30 pm. Individuals can also ask questions and have them answered by the rangers. This is a fantastic way for your children to learn more about South African wildlife and flora and fauna.

Crafts

Crafts provide endless ways to keep your family entertained during lockdown. Pinterest and Instagram offer a wealth of ideas of crafts to do with your children regardless of their age or interests. Many of these exercises are ideal for learning, problem-solving as well as important in the development of fine motor skills in smaller children.

Gardening

Whether you have a garden, balcony, or backyard, gardening is an ideal activity for both parents and children. While trying to minimize your trips to the grocery store, plant some herbs and vegetables that you can use in your daily cooking. Growing herbs and vegetables is also a fantastic educational opportunity for children. In addition to teaching them responsibility, gardening is an ideal activity to reduce stress, frustration, and anxiety.

Create a scavenger hunt

A scavenger hunt is an ideal way for keeping small children (or older kids if they still have a sense of adventure) entertained. You can even encourage your kids to create their hunts to promote creativity and out-the-box thinking. Decorate areas of your home with little surprises and develop clues for children to guess where things are hidden.

Socialize virtually

The popularity of apps such as House party and Zoom have skyrocketed in the face of social distancing. Instead of putting social events like Friday night drinks, family lunches, and playdates on hold, these apps are helping people of all ages stay connected and retain their social lives during isolation. For the extroverts among us, this is a critical way of staying entertained during a lockdown.

Create home obstacle courses

This is one of the more creative ways to keep your family entertained during a lockdown. Children need to burn off some of those seemingly endless energy supplies. Unfortunately, with parks and playgrounds closed, parents need to get creative. Obstacle courses are a fun way to keep your children active. Get creative and use various household objects, including dining chairs, cushions, boxes, and tables. Create obstacles for kids to climb, go under, wind around, crawl through, and jump.

Knitting

It's not just for little old ladies. Knitting has experienced a resurgence in popularity in recent years, with many younger people embracing the activity. The monotony of wielding those needles has also been known to lower one's heart rate and reduce harmful blood levels of the stress hormone cortisol (source). Set a family goal to create blankets to donate to the less fortunate in preparation for the upcoming winter months.

Decluttering is a way to keep your family entertained during the lockdown

. All this extra time at home makes it an ideal time for decluttering and tidying. This is a cathartic and mood-boosting activity that the whole family can get involved in. Make the tasks fun by encouraging each person to go through their drawers and cupboards, and create piles of what will be donated, sold, and thrown away.

REFERENCES

Barkley, R.A. (2000) Taking Charge of ADHD: The Complete, Authoritative Guide for Parents.

Brown T.E. (2005) Attention Deficit Disorder: The Unfocused Mind in Children and Adults.

Greene, R.W. (2005) The Explosive Child.

Quinn, P. (2001) ADD and the College Student: A Guide for High School and College Students with Attention Deficit Disorder (revised).

Quinn, P. and Stern, J. (2001) Putting on the Brakes: Young People's Guide to Understanding Attention Deficit Hyperactivity Disorder (revised).

Smith, B.H., Barkley, R.A. and Shapiro, C.J. (2006) "Attention-deficit/ hyperactivity disorder." In E. Mash and R. Barkley (eds) Treatment of Childhood Disorders (3rd edn).

Waslick, B. and Greenhill, L. (2004) "Attention deficit/hyperactivity disorder."

J. Wiener and M. Dulcan (eds). Textbook of Child and Adolescent Psychiatry (3rd edn).

Zeigler Dendy, C. (2006) Teenagers with ADD and ADHD: A Guide for Parents and Professionals.

Vincent J. Monastra. Ph.D. (2014) Parenting Children with ADHD 10 Lessons That Medicine Cannot Teach.

Cindy Goldrich. 8 Keys to Parenting Children with ADHD.

Elizabeth A. Laugeson, Psy.D. The Science of Making Friends: Helping Socially Challenged Teens and Young Adults.

Fred Frankel, Ph.D. Friends Forever: How Parents Can Help Their Kids Make and Keep Good Friends.

Linda Carroll. "Kids with ADHD May Be More Likely to Bully." NBC News. (2008). Web. (http://www.nbcnews.com/id/22813400/ns/health-childrens_health/t/kids-adhd- may-be-more-likely-bully/#.VtmuU_krK70).

Neurological basis for ADHD, A. Singer, E. Technology Review (August 9, 2007).
(http://www.technologyreview.com/Biotech/19197/).

Barkley, R. A, 2006. Attention Deficit Hyperactive Disorder: A Handbook for Diagnosis and Treatment.

Jackson, Luke. A User Guide to the GF/CF Diet for Autism, Asperger Syndrome and ADHD.

If you enjoyed reading "Side Effect of the New Normal" by Meredith Alexander than visit our website: mindfullyfresh.com and subscribe to our monthly newsletter and other free resources.

You'll also enjoy other books available on Amazon and other book resellers worldwide:

Calmer Kids in 7 Minutes or Less: Activity Book (Mindfulness for Children)

Calmer Kids in 7 Minutes or Less: Unabridged Version (Mindfulness for Children)

Self-Care Isn't Selfish: Self Care Activity Book

Self-Care Isn't Selfish Journal

Peace and Clarity Activity Book

Peace and Clarity Unabridged Version

Perfectly Imperfect Activity Book (Mindfulness for Teen Girls)

Perfectly Imperfect Unabridged Version (Mindfulness for Teen Girls)

Emoji Journal

Emoji Journal Spanish

Gratitude Journal

MindfullyFresh Journal

MindfullyFresh Kids Journal

The Devils We Know: Activity Book to Combat Gaslighting and Other Manipulative Tactics

There are a host of courses that will help you on your quest to mindfulness. With the goal of taking bettser care of yourself and then taking better care of those around you!

Thank You,

Meredith Alexander

*Disclaimer our material (books, courses, newsletters, blogs, etc.) are strictly for information and entertainment purposes. We strongly recommend specialized help with a doctor and therapist to help you achieve your mental health goals!

www.ingramcontent.com/pod-product-compliance
Lightning Source LLC
Chambersburg PA
CBHW031414040426
42444CB00005B/563